NORMATIVE PSYCHOANALYSIS

Scholarly Articles by Peter Fritz Walter

The Law of Evidence

The Restriction of National Sovereignty

Alternative Medicine and Wellness Techniques

Consciousness and Shamanism

Creative Prayer

Soul Jazz

The Ego Matter

The Star Script

The Lunar Bull

Basics of Mythology

Basics of Feng Shui

Power or Depression?

The Mythology of Narcissism

Normative Psychoanalysis

Notes on Consciousness

Patterns of Perception

Sane Child vs. Insane Society

Basics of the Science of Mind

The Secret Science

Oedipal Hero

Processed Reality

NORMATIVE
PSYCHOANALYSIS

HOW THE OEDIPAL DOGMA SHAPES
CONSUMER CULTURE

BY PETER FRITZ WALTER

Published by Sirius-C Media Galaxy LLC
Business Filings Incorporated
108 West 13th St., Wilmington, DE 19801

Set in Trajan Pro and ITC Berkeley Oldstyle Std

Designed by Peter Fritz Walter

Publishing Categories
Psychology / Psychotherapy / Child & Adolescent

Publisher Contact Information
publisher@sirius-c-publishing.com
http://sirius-c-publishing.com

Author Contact Information
pfw@peterfritzwalter.com

About Dr. Peter Fritz Walter
http://peterfritzwalter.com

About the Author

Parallel to an international law career in Germany, Switzerland and the United States, Dr. Peter Fritz Walter (Pierre) focused upon fine art, cookery, astrology, musical performance, social sciences and humanities.

He started writing essays as an adolescent and received a high school award for creative writing and editorial work for the school magazine.

After finalizing his law diplomas, he graduated with an LL.M. in European Integration at Saarland University, Germany, and with a Doctor of Law title from University of Geneva, Switzerland, in 1987.

He then took courses in psychology at the University of Geneva and interviewed a number of psychotherapists in Lausanne and Geneva, Switzerland. His interest was intensified through a hypnotherapy with an Ericksonian American hypnotherapist in Lausanne. This led him to the recovery and healing of his inner child.

In 1986, he met the late French psychotherapist and child psychoanalyst Françoise Dolto (1908-1988) in Paris and interviewed her. A long correspondence followed up to their encounter which was considered by the curators of the Dolto

Trust interesting enough to be published in a book alongside all of Dolto's other letter exchanges by Gallimard Publishers in Paris, in 2005.

After a second career as a corporate trainer and personal coach, Pierre retired as a full-time writer, philosopher and consultant.

His nonfiction books emphasize a systemic, holistic, cross-cultural and interdisciplinary perspective, while his fiction works and short stories focus upon education, philosophy, perennial wisdom, and the poetic formulation of an integrative worldview.

Pierre is a German-French bilingual native speaker and writes English as his 4th language after German, Latin and French. He also reads source literature for his research works in Spanish, Italian, Portuguese, and Dutch. In addition, Pierre has notions of Thai, Khmer, Chinese and Japanese.

All of Pierre's books are hand-crafted and self-published, designed by the author. Pierre publishes via his Delaware company, Sirius-C Media Galaxy LLC, and under the imprints of IPUBLICA and SCM (Sirius-C Media).

CONTENTS

Dedicated to the late Françoise Dolto (1908-1988) who so far was the one and only professional to correctly understand my activism for the cause of the child.

CHAPTER ONE

The Consumer Child's Entanglement

L et me first elucidate why I came to research these hairy issues of codependence and emotional abuse after having
started, back in 1985, a much vaster research
project on the topic of physical and sexual violence
against children.

It was a coincidental if not synchronistic real-
life event that brought me to switch focus, after
about three months of intensive research. I found
first of all that while violence against children and
sexual abuse of children were topics already well-
covered by forensic science and psychology, there
was at the time as good as nothing to be found
about emotional abuse.

But that alone would probably not have got me
on what I consider today is the right track; it was
encounters with adolescents during my research

work in the United States that got me to rethink my initial research proposition, and open up to what I simply had overlooked—and symptomatically so because I myself was emotionally abused over the entire course of my childhood and youth, and even still as a young adult.

Once I had discovered the new path for my research, I was not taking long to understand that there is something like a gradual relationship between codependence and emotional abuse, that both etiologies are sharing a common root in that emotional abuse is but the higher octave of parent-child codependence, the worsening of a pathological condition that in most cases goes unnoticed and is yet detrimental to the child growing into autonomy and self-reliance.

Let me emphasize here that my definition of codependence slightly differs from mainstream research for the simple reason that I specialized from the start upon parent-child codependence, while the problem usually is discussed more in terms of partnership codependence, the problem that in a couple relation one of the partners projects their parent of the opposite sex upon the other partner with the result that sexual relations will be rendered impossible sooner or later.

Needless to add that parent-child codependence is way more devastating for the child than this may be the case for any of the partners in a codependent marriage or concubinage, simply because children's biosystem is so much softer than that of an adult, and can thus more easily be imprinted with behavior patterns that, good or not, later will form the overall behavior of the person.

For example, a man who was for the whole of his childhood codependent with his mother, while the father was absent, will always have conflictual relations with women, if he will have relations with women at all, and not later on opt for relations with little girls or boys, in order to circumvent the 'incest injunction' rendered by his inner critic that acts under the spell of what I came to call the 'Oedipal Cognitive Confusion.'

It is important to understand that codependence and emotional abuse, while they are treated under two different headers, are two poles of the same psychic complex, which is why I discuss

them here in one and the same study. As a side re-
mark, let me add here that I discuss parent-child
codependence synonymously under the headers of
cofusion, secondary fusion, pseudo-fusion, and
symbiotoholism, terms I have forged myself and
that I find more descriptive than the term 'codependence.'

It is by an large a dependency problem that
manifests in the parent-child relation typically for
the first time after the critical mother-infant symbiosis, and thus as a general rule after the 18th
month of the newborn.

What is generally little known is the fact that
even before the completion of the 18th month of
the infant, mother and child are interacting in a
subtle communication about limits which reveals
to what extent the mother is able and willing to
give the infant autonomy, or not. This early dialogue, that is most of the time nonverbal, has been
found to deeply condition people for their later relational behavior patterns.

This is more true in the mother-son relation
than it is in the father-daughter relation simply be-

cause the matrix-provider has more conditioning power over the child, be it boy or girl, than the sperm-giver.

This evaluation of the primal scene has been found valid both by Freudian psychoanalysis and Transactional Analysis (TA), and it is not as such a matter of cultural conditioning, or compliance to either matriarchy or patriarchy.

Codependence is a major building block in the political and social entanglement scheme of what I call *Oedipal Culture*. Causative factors that have been revealed in my own and other research are:

> ▸ Mother did not really want the child;

> ▸ Mother cares more about her career than her baby;

> ▸ Lack of healthy parent-child physical interaction;

> ▸ Parents leaving the child to babysitters most of the time;

> ▸ Insufficient eye contact in the mother-infant relation;

> ▸ Insufficient or no breastfeeding;

▸ Mother was breastfeeding but felt revulsion;

▸ Infant tactile deprivation syndrome;

▸ Shame-based identity of the mother and resulting rejection behavior:

- when baby shows erotic behavior, and mother turns away regard;

- when baby touches his or her genitals, and mother takes their hands off;

- when baby seeks closeness with mother, and mother puts baby to sleep;

- when mother holds the baby constantly away from her body, to avoid touch and being touched;

- when mother constantly has 'no time' for baby and admonishes baby to be 'not so demanding;'

- etc.

▸ Father left wife and child during pregnancy, after birth or not long thereafter;

▸ Father, while still part of the family, is as good as never present, alcoholic or practices progeny;

▸ Father refuses to take over any role in childcare;

▸ Father is abusive toward mother and/or child, etc.

In other words, codependence is a compensation reaction of entangled organisms that intends
to heal a split that was caused by a lack of early intimacy. The entanglement paradoxically comes
about through a lack of physical closeness, and of
communication, and through general tactile deprivation of the child, and also through non-physical
elements such as parents' thoughts being constantly focused on money and status or children generally relegated to receiving affection from secondary
caretakers, nurses, babysitters, house teachers, and
the like.

The entanglement specifically comes about
through the fact of lacking autonomy of the child,
and of lacking exposure to experiences and a social
life outside of the family.

Details have been shown with abundant evidence by the long-term research of James W.
Prescott, Ashley Montagu, Michel Odent, Frederick
Leboyer, Melanie Klein, Alexander Lowen and others.

The problem of codependence is for obvious
reasons much more stringent in the individualistic

and separative white Western cultures than in highly sociable open societies such as African, South American or Asian cultures. Yet in these cultures we face the problem in the middle and upper classes today as well because they have adopted Western values and a lifestyle that clones most of the alienated Western behavior models, thereby shunning their own perennial wisdom that their elders still are knowledgeable about.

There are many myths that distort and tear down naturally erotic but nonsexual relations between parents and children, and these distorted popular views actually foster and purport codependence instead of helping to avoid it. For example, contrary to popular belief, the pathological codependence between parent and child is not the result of too much physical interaction and shared affection and tenderness, but in the contrary through touch hostility and prudishness. It has often been believed that a boy will develop a codependent relationship with his mother when he is 'too close' to her, or when he sleeps with his mother in the same bed. This is simply not true.

The causes of mother-son codependence are often depicted in an overly simplified or even distorted manner. To begin with, it is not through abundant shared pleasure, affection, tenderness, and body touch that codependence is brought about. It's not through mother and son, or father and daughter, sleeping together, taking baths together, sharing nudity, and it's not through their sharing a naturally sensual and erotic attraction for each other.

In the contrary, if these elements were causative factors in the etiology of codependence, any abundantly sensual mothering or fathering would lead to entrapping children in pseudo-incestuous relations. But this is not the case. If a mother is fully erotically present for her boy-child, without being incestuous, and embraces him sensually while giving him at the same time the necessary amount of autonomy according to his age and abilities, the boy will easily master the *Oedipus Complex* and develop his fully functional heterosexuality; he will then project his libido upon peer girls of his age, or approximately of his age. The same is true in the father-daughter relation with regard to the girl-child's mastering the Electra Complex and projecting her sexual feelings upon peers boys.

There are many false signals in today's popular culture and vulgarized psychological publications. These false signals lead to parents' becoming more and more insecure as to the role physical affection and sensual touch play in healthy parenting. This makes that parents are more or less constantly bombarded with ambiguous messages with the consequence that many parents retreat physically from their children, thereby inclosing them in atrocious feelings of abandonment, loneliness and despair.

As a result of 1960s American pediatrics that advocated physical separation between parents and child which in the meantime is seen as a fundamental error, many of today's parents had a deprivatory childhood themselves and became dysfunctional parents of their own children.

Fact is that it is through the absence of the father together with a shame-based identification process in the mother-son relation that mother-son codependence is brought about. The reason for the

more dramatic constellation in the mother-son relation has to do with the greater psychic fragility of
the human male in general, and with the simple
fact that it's the mother who is the matrix, not the
father, in particular.

If we want to add one more problem complex
here it's the codependent mother-daughter relation.
By contrast, father-child care in our culture is sel-
dom codependent simply because the father is
most of the time absent. And this is, then, also one
of the causative factors in mother-son codependence. Apart from this, there are singular cases of
father-daughter codependence and they are
marked by the fact that the father exceedingly
overprotects the girl-child to an extent to virtually
keep her 'away from life.'

As I have seen it in many families, this can
bring about absurd constellations and relationships
that symbolically express that the child is no more
allowed to walk on their own feet, but on the feet
of the father, so as to be 'protected of the harshness
of life.' The problem is much more manifest in
white American culture than in black American

culture, or any of non-Western and tribal (native) cultures for that matter.

My research has shown that virtually the only cultures that do *not* have the problem are tribal cultures, that is most native populations around the world.

One important element in this etiology, that has hardly been elucidated by modern research, is that these children experience dreadful and lasting loneliness during their whole childhood and youth.

Another important insight about mother-child codependence is that it deprives the child, typically the boy, of the time and care needed for developing his true intelligence, his own intrinsic gifts and talents.

Men who grow up entangled with their mothers are caught in a net of stiffening responsibilities, or obligations, or what is felt as such, which impedes them from really thinking of themselves, and minding their own business.

The result is that they hardly think their projects through to the end, taking time and rest for vision-building, constantly harassed by their demanding mothers, threatened with love denial or even financial starving in case they disobey and begin to live their own lives.

In this sense, it can be said that the son bears the cross for the sins committed by his mother, and it's really a capital sin to suffocate a young man's energies and intelligence by throwing one's weight around as a mother and disregarding his fragility as a man. In this sense, many women in our society need to be educated what right motherhood is about, and even more so, what wrong motherhood is.

Not only is the mother-entangled man subject to ridicule and humiliation, he is also one of the major actors on the stage of child-focused sexual crime.

Our mass media depict the truth in a distorted manner, suggesting with their politically correct rhetoric a boy had to care for his mom eternally, if he's a 'good boy.' These views have to be judged perverse, as they are really putting nature upside down. Childhood is transitory. Period.

The French child psychoanalyst and therapist Françoise Dolto (1908-1988) has analyzed this problem in the mother-son relation, in her book *Psychanalyse et Pédiatrie (1971)*, and she writes:

> There are boys who stay lovingly fixated upon their mothers; their behavior is characterized by the fact that they do not attempt to 'seduce' any other woman. If the father is alive, the two men are constantly disputing, for the fact that the boy does not detach himself from his mother and searches out other love and sex objects proves that the boy has not liquidated—in a friendship of equality with his father—his pre-oedipal homosexuality. He will therefore prepare for getting 'in trouble' with his father through his difficult and provocative behavior. (Translation mine)

> When the father has left and the boy 'dedicates himself' to his mother, this behavior can be accompanied by real social sublimations, which are associated with the activities derived from the repression of genital and procreative sexuality, but this boy cannot behave sexually and affectively like an adult. He suffers from inferiority feelings toward men that he unconsciously identifies with his father; he can also be a hyper-genital who is always avid to get new sex partners toward whom he will never build real attachment, but he will show impotent in relations with any woman he really loves, because this is associated in his unconscious with the tabooed incestuous object. (Id., 88, Translation mine)

The messages those boys and young men are typically bombarded with are, for example:

—You are egoistic

—You are like your father …

—Think a little of your mother …

—I'm always sitting at home, can't you make time and show me around a little?

—You should have more gratitude for your mother, etc.

And when the boy is on the right track and really develops a unique genuine interest, mother will have enough reasons to tell him that he's inadequate for it:

—Why do you spend so much time for this, it leads nowhere …

—Stay with your feet on the ground, you have grandiose ideas …

—Like your father, big mouth and little wisdom …

—Others have done that before you, so where's the sense of it?

—You better spend your time taking care of your old mother!

—Why don't you follow my advice, you are just stubborn.

—I always told you, but you know everything better …

Much evil in the world done by men has its roots in a stiffening mother-son relation that deprives the young boy for years of his vital energies, blocking his emotional flow to a point of self-forgetfulness. This is, then, the reason why these men one day explode, so to speak, for thinking of themselves for one time, and do something horrible, to a woman, a little girl, or an elder. And who goes to jail is always the boy, then a man, and not his mother. And that, in my humble opinion, should be changed. Women are to be made responsible for being abusive as mothers, not only men, as fathers! Women always claim to not being given enough responsibility under patriarchy, but most women bluntly deny their abusive attitudes toward their sons in our society, which is an abuse of responsibility, an abuse of power. However, this abuse is hidden for the most part, and often veiled behind feminist activism, a career or what I came to call a victim attitude. Women always cry for abuse when it's about them, never when it's about the sons they drive into madness, suicide, child rape or even murder. And here our criminal laws have definitely to be changed, definitely!

Of course, in the clinical and psychotherapeutic practice, codependence does not in the first place manifest as a parent-child problem, but as a husband-spouse problem, and that is why it comes up in marriage counseling and family therapy. And that is exactly what makes it so intricate and difficult to heal it in the therapeutic setting.

What many practitioners overlook is that the problem does not originate in the partner relation but in the earlier parent-child relations that both partners went through and that they project, as a matter of unconscious automatisms, upon their partner. We all project our parent of the opposite sex upon our spouse or husband, only that there are two essentially different ways of doing that, a conscious way based on the letting-go of the parent (mourning), or an unconscious way based on entanglement, confusion and hate-love.

In the Freudian terminology of the *Oedipus Complex*, the first alternative corresponds to what Freud called a liquidated Oedipus and the second corresponds to what Freud called an unresolved Oedipus.

Christopher Bagley writes in his book *Child Abusers: Research and Treatment (2003)*:

> Emotional abuse causes the most long-term harm to children, although combinations of emotional with physical and/or sexual abuse cause the most harm to long-term mental health.

But what is emotional abuse, emotional incest or covert incest? I think that today many men have a quite sadistic relationship with women, which is something like a revenge reaction or compensation for the codependence they went through with their mothers. Unconsciously, these men want to punish their mothers for the constant humiliations, the constant withdrawal of affection, the conditioned love they received and the painful lack of autonomy that is the sad reality in this kind of exclusive relationships.

The main problem in our culture is the mother-son relation and as good as all our social and relational problems flow out from this major distortion. Many men project their controversial feelings toward their mothers later on their spouses, girlfriends, and even little girls they encounter, with the result that the ambiguous, ambivalent, and hardly conscious feelings of aggression they bear against their mothers is projected outward in society, and creates havoc in man-woman and man-girl relationships.

This aggression in men comes about through the combination of lacking autonomy in their boyhood, absence of the father, demanding attitude of the mother for the son to stay at home, strict education with frequent humiliating punishment, isolation from peers through motherly overprotection, attitude to enclose the boy in an exclusive, intimate and emotionally abusive relation, victim attitude of the mother, and the explicit or hidden demonization of the boy's peer relations, friendships and social life.

A way out could be a certain persistence of the boy in the face of such a situation, and a firmness to be developed on his part that insists on his right to maintain relationships with peers, teens and adults other than tutelary figures and family, and that he asks for a certain laps of free time, every weekend, for going out alone, and unmonitored. This could give the young male the opportunity to speak about his emotional pressures, about the humiliation he suffers and his confused feelings, especially when the boy turns into adolescence and these feelings of aggression begin to get sexualized and become more or less violent sexual urges. While generally, with overprotected youngsters, a problem of acceptance will occur at the beginning in any group relation and a certain hostility may be experienced at the start, it can only be beneficial for young people to leave their nest from time to time to search out peer company and also adult males and females, who may be in state to support the young boy in his rightful quest for autonomy and respect.

The advice that I give is to strengthen personal autonomy, and to get into an inner dialogue with the shadow, and the inner child, in order to unveil the hidden distortions in the mother-son relation that has been internalized and that can be gradually rendered conscious through this kind of work.

The result of my now thirty years of research on abuse and sexual paraphilias is that these sexual distortions result from mother-son codependence that has reached a level of gravity to be qualified as emotional abuse, and which is to be seen as one of the biggest relational problems of our times.

Unfortunately, Western psychiatry only very recently began to get a hint of the emotional abuse pathology; to repeat it, when I started my research, back in 1985, there was not yet any book published on the matter, while emotional abuse now is considered as the worst and most long-term form of abuse, as it's of all abuse etiologies the primary etiology.

Sexual abuse is only one of several consequences of emotional abuse. Emotional abuse has become something like my research specialty and even now, I discovered, relatively few books are published about it, while whole libraries have been written on sexual abuse and father-daughter incest.

Contrary to many psychiatrists, I came to believe through my research that the long-term psychic strain and fixations sexual abuse causes is not typically related to the sexual experience, if there was any, but to the following factors that are, or are not, present in such cases:

—Suddenness of the experience;

—Behavior of the adult was in conflict with social code or family attitude;

—Entrapment effect that led to immediate anxiety;

—Debasing attitude of the man of the type 'I can have all females I want';

—Impossibility to speak up, even after the experience, that is, a general milieu that would endanger the child to talk to anybody about the experience.

Much could be changed if anti-abuse social work could be based on these research insights instead of going on with tearing in the dirt certain forms of sexuality, as this is the common public rhetoric in today's postmodern international consumer culture.

The focus is obviously wrong, as authors such as Stevi Jackson, a feminist activist, and Alayne Yates, an American child psychologist, have shown in their books.

—See Stevi Jackson, Childhood and Sexuality (1982) and Alayne Yates, Sex Without Shame: Encouraging Your Child's Healthy Sexual Development (1978).

The focus must be on fighting coercion, violence, and entrapment, not sexuality, and Western society should eventually learn to accept all forms of sexual behavior as a non-vulgar, non-harmful, non-debasing and creative human activity. Sexuality, after all, is a form of communication, and it's a social, not an asocial activity.

Together with sexual prudishness, what Western culture does in addition is to distort and pervert children's emotional life virtually from the cradle, and the Freudian myth of the *Oedipus Complex* has contributed to this distortion of the natural psychosexual growth of the child.

Children do not grow through being codependent ersatz partners of their parents, and yet this is exactly what the present culture is doing with them, imprisoning them in the nuclear family and depriving them of the whole bunch of hairy folk they were hitherto exposed to, when still growing up in the extended family and also a good part of the day living in the street, without being constantly monitored and followed up.

The present structure virtually breeds violence, and this on a worldwide scale because the Western educational paradigm is exported all over the world within global consumer culture.

Chapter Two

The Oedipal Mold

What means 'Oedipus Complex?'

Sigmund Freud (1856–1939), an Austrian neurologist and co-founder of the psychoanalytic school of psychology believed that psychosexual growth comes in three stages, the so-called *oral phase (0 to 2 years), anal phase (2 to 4 years)* and *genital phase (4 to 7 years)*, followed by the *latency period (7 to 11 years)* and *adolescence (11 to 16 years)* and that the child invariably passes through these stages.

—I have oversimplified the age groups here for easier understanding; in reality the borderline between the phases is not that clear-cut. Most psychoanalysts, for example, let the oral phase end with the age of 18 months of the infant, and put this also as the ideal end of the primary symbiosis with the mother. In addition, it has to be seen that children are not automatons and do not follow those schemes on the letter, which is especially true for highly gifted children. It is known, to give an example out of context, that the late pianist Arthur Rubinstein did not speak before the age of three, but he spoke at once several languages.

In addition, Freud argued that the intrinsic set-up of the sexual drive structure was taking place through *identifications*, especially the identification, during the anal phase, with the parent of the same sex, that Freud called *homosexual identification* and the following *heterosexual identification* with the parent of the opposite sex, during the genital phase.

This latter sprocket in the psychosexual process of sexual growth was called *Oedipus Complex* by Freud.

More specifically Freud and later psychoanalysis require the child to successfully liquidate each phase or fixation, and conclude that if a child was not able to do such liquidation, the sexual energy would become stuck in the particular phase where the development was arrested with poignant consequences on sexual habits.

For example it is argued that when a child does not successfully liquidate the *Oedipus Complex* by developing a strong heterosexual relationship with the parent of the opposite sex (without however acting this attraction out as incest), then the child was likely to become homosexual later on. Freud has found this first for boys with regard to their mother, and later added it on for the girl-father relationship, which he called *Electra Complex*.

Is the Oedipus Complex Universal?

I think a number of intelligent and child-loving people find it makes sense when Freud affirmed the *basic sexual nature* of the child and infantile sexuality. But my question is if this understanding really implies that they see and acknowledge Western culture's fundamental denial of the child's affective, emotional and sexual complexity?

As a parent, to allow one's child to be sexual in a culture that actually is against that kind of freedom, really is a challenge; that is why only when parents get the whole picture, they can do what needs to be done. If parents are wishy-washy on this question, and half-hearted, it makes it probably only worse.

When I was starting my research, I honestly had no idea that children could have an authentic sexual life in the sense of engaging in penetratory embrace, not just in the sense of being autoerotic through masturbation or mutual masturbation with a friend. I learnt these facts through anthropological field work, ethnological reports published by Bronislaw Malinowski, Margaret Mead, and others, and through literature on alternative childhood, and children in the counter-culture.

> —See, for example, Bronislaw Malinowski, The Sexual Life of Savages in North West Melanesia (1929) and Sex and Repression in Savage Society (1927/1985), Margaret Mead, Sex and Temperament in Three Primitive Societies (1935), Susanne Cho, Kindheit und Sexualität im Wandel der Kulturgeschichte (1983), Larry L. & Joan M. Constantine, Treasures of the Island: Children in Alternative Lifestyles (1976) and Where Are the Kids? (1977), V. Elwin, The Muria and their Ghotul (1947), Richard L. Currier, Juvenile Sexuality in Global Perspective, in : Children & Sex, New Findings, New Perspectives (1981), pp. 9 ff.

In the absence of this vital and important knowledge, Freud's theory that children's psychosexual development is a process of libidinal identifications was for me an attractive surrogate for the real knowledge!

And it is an attractive lie, for it justifies the existence of the holy consumer family with a child as the main stage clown who is used and abused under the pretext of his or her 'infantile' needs— while the reality is that this psychological construct rather serves the the parents' needs for emotional security and the socially sanctified and legally imposed avoidance of children's *real autonomy* through real erotic experience with people outside of the nuclear family.

The myth of 'infantile sexuality' is obviously a reductionist and pseudo-scientific cover-up needed by today's mainstream child psychology to continue their blinding out the fact that the child is a complete human from birth! It could appropriately be called child sex mythology! Freud was the avatar for what later became, and today still is, the mainstream paradigm in child psychology and education.

One of the pitfalls of our modern educational system is the exclusion and societal blinding out of parameters that serve to build identity through self-knowledge, intuitive or inner knowledge, paranormal knowledge, pre-life knowledge and relational experience. The identity that is said to be the only possible mold according to Western mainstream psychiatry is a derived, not a genuine, identity. It is derived from the parents' identities.

For a boy, for example, the process will be identification with the father, as primary homosexual identification, during the anal phase and identification with the mother, as secondary heterosexual identification during the genital phase. True identity is built, according to this system, when the boy has successfully liquidated the *Oedipus Complex* by having developed enough aggression against the father and enough castration of his incestuous desire toward the mother at the same time.

That this system is built upon the grave of child sexuality, in the sense of *child-child sexual activity* is clear from the start. It was clear to Freud but he thought that a deeper yielding to the core of nature's laws would throw Western bourgeoisie into chaos.

I critically reviewed Freud's theory of infantile sexuality and came to the conclusion that Freud's scheme is clearly detrimental to the child's building autonomy, by keeping the consumer child in pseudo-fusional dependence on their parents, thus creating codependence and perversion, and a fake heterosexuality that covers up all the undealt-with secondary drives that are produced by forcefully impeding the child from living out their natural emosexual attraction toward peers.

My wake up call had come not from psychology, but from the side of anthropology and the insights I got through my studies of the human energy field, the energetic functionality of the organism and the nature of the bioenergy.

> —See Peter Fritz Walter, The Energy Nature of Human Emotions and Sexual Attraction: A Systemic Analysis of Emotional Identity in the Human Sexual Response, 2015/2017.

It was first of all through the anthropological findings of Bronislaw Malinowski and Margaret Mead and their observations of biologically healthy child-child sexuality with the Melanesian Trobriand culture, and other tribal cultures, that brought about a change in my regard upon child sexuality.

We have two ways to create a new reality, in which society, recognizing the child's affective, emotional and sexual complexity and high bioenergetic charge, sets up new and comprehensive forms of child-rearing:

▸ by confining the child in an oedipal triangle within the nuclear family, depriving them of non-incestuous erotic relations, and thereby artificially raising their gerontophilic eroticism, while projecting this eroticism exclusively upon the parents, and in turn creating a striking conflict within the child's psychosomatic setup;

or

▸ by transforming mainstream culture and granting children their own domain of intimacy, outside of the parent's embrace, allowing the child to live their affective, emotional and sexual complexity in freedom, thus helping the child to build true autonomy and self-reliance.

The first alternative leads to the consumer child. The second alternative leads to a complete human.

To summarize, Sigmund Freud has significantly contributed to consolidating what I call *Oedipal Culture*, to a point to have prepared the subtle ideological soil for postmodern international consumer culture. Freud has less significantly contributed to helping the modern child consolidating their natural quest for autonomy and self-reliance, and their birthright for an *unobserved realm of intimacy,* outside of the jovially persecutory parental and educational embrace, if not to be kept save from the Kindergarten regime of slave-puppets to their culturally perverted and schizoid parents and educators.

CRITICISM OF THE THEORY

I present my critique of Freud's theory of the *Oedipus Complex* here in eight distinct points.

RESTRICTED VALIDITY

The Freudian scheme of 'infantile sexuality' is only if ever valid for cultures where child-child erotic relations are forbidden and structurally impaired, that is, for patriarchal culture and postmodern international consumer culture as the successor, in a new garment, of the patriarchal rut;

CULTURAL CONDITIONING TOWARD HOMOSEXUALITY

The Freudian scheme represents systematic perversion of the child and implies the cultural conditioning toward homosexuality because identification is not the natural way for the child to build his drive structure, and to individuate, but a culturally conditioned one, which is why I call this culture also *Hero Culture*, implying the child is molded after their parents taken as cultural standard molds, and not in relation to their own specific soul structure, and emotional setup.

A DISTORTED PSYCHOSEXUAL BASE STRUCTURE

Building homosexual attraction *before* building heterosexual attraction is not the way nature builds our psychosexual structure, but is a pure projection upon nature. Small boys are erotically attracted to their mothers and girls to their fathers, and not homosexually toward their same-sex parents. This is so from birth, not just from age four or five, as the Freudian myth assumes. When, as this is admittedly often the case within patriarchal cultures, children are well homosexually fixated upon their same-sex parent, and refuse to open up for embracing their parent of the opposite sex, exhibiting anxiety in front of anything erotic, this is so because the child is narcissistic and neurotic. Needless to add that the neurotic child is of course not the natural child; when this happens, it has a reason, as it does not happen with children who are educated with love.

I have personally seen it over and over with children whose parent of the same sex gives only *conditioned* love, and where children lack emotional constancy and security with their parents, or even grow in disruptive and dysfunctional families.

MECHANISTIC VIEW OF SEXUALITY

Freud's professional and private life philosophy was patriarchal and at the same time materialistic, and mechanistic. He had discarded out of his life any spirituality as well as his wistful Jewish tradition, and most of his theories defy truly spiritual insights and truths. The very essence of a holistic worldview, that sees the *hidden connections* was alien to Freud. This was one of the reasons that his relational life was full of strife and disruption, and ended in many painful separations and personal conflicts.

It can be said, *cum grano salis*, that Freud was abandoned later in his life by all his real friends, which was one element in the etiology of his atrociously painful death of jaw cancer.

When we consider that we are talking about love, and erotic attraction, when we talk about the psychosexual growth of the child, it denotes confusion to choose Freud as the authority on the matter. He was not. That Freud's theories are slavishly followed till today has political reasons, and is in no way to attribute to any real insights he had. In fact, Freud's psychosexual theories are the ideological base justification for the enslavement of the consumer child, with all that results from this cultural perversion.

Nature Fosters Copulation, Not Masturbation

Freud overlooked not only female sexuality, as the feminist movement rightfully alleges, but he also overlooked that the small child is not an auto-erotic freak and serial masturbator when being allowed to have full relations with other children. Freud ignored the *real* natural emotional and sexual growth processes in children, as they are amply demonstrated by non-patriarchal cultures where children enjoy full sexual freedom from early childhood. In these cultures, children engage in sexual peer relations that are tolerated and encouraged, but not interfered with by tutelary adults, as shown by the ample research of Bronislaw Malinowski, Margaret Mead and Wilhelm Reich, and many others.

—See Bronislaw Malinowski, Crime and Custom in Savage Society (1926), Sex and Repression in Savage Society (1927), The Sexual Life of Savages in North West Melanesia (1929), Margaret Mead, Sex and Temperament in Three Primitive Societies (1935), Floyd M. Martinson, Infant and Child Sexuality (1973), The Quality of Adolescent Experiences (1974), The Sex Education of Young Children, in: Lorna Brown (Ed.), Sex Education in the Eighties (1981), The Sexual Life of Children (1994), Children and Sex, Part II: Childhood Sexuality, in: Bullough & Bullough, Human Sexuality (1994), and Wilhelm Reich, Children of the Future (1950).

THE 'OEDIPAL FAMILY' BRINGS PERVERSION, NOT SANITY

Freud's system reflects the power structures of patriarchal society; he just put names on things that were already there. In fact, today's global consumer society is unthinkable without the conditioning dogma of the *Oedipus Complex*, the resulting parent-child codependence and the confusion it brings about in the mind of the child. Truly, when natural peer relations are forbidden to the child and because autonomy and self-thinking abilities of the child are replaced to a large extent by system-conform consumer conditioning, the way is open for total addiction in form of non-ending consumption. The result is the perverse consumer child, and the so-called citizen, that are both based on the massacre of the original primal child that was naturally heterosexual—and more generally so, *sexual* in the first place.

The Oedipal Theory is Pseudo-Science

The theory of the *polymorphously perverse infant* that was erected by Freud is a result of the mechanistic science tradition along the lines of Jean-Jacques Rousseau, La Mettrie, Baron d'Holbach, René Descartes and others, which considered man being a machine and infants to be born as a *tabula rasa*. While this view today is scientifically outdated and while we know that infants are born with a full heritage of former incarnations and resulting imprints in the soul, positivistic modern child-psychology has to this day not done the necessary shift from a blind mechanistic and highly doctrinaire pseudo-science into a real holistic science of the bioenergy. I have created this science and call it *Emonics (Emotional Identity Code Science)*. Emonics assumes that our emotional identity is a soul imprint, which is the blueprint of our later individuality. It also assumes that all in life is a function of the human energy field or quantum vacuum. Sexuality is but flowing vital energy and has little to do with the mechanistic assumptions ignorant sexology and doctrinaire psychology as well as myth-ridden psychoanalysis projected upon it.

—See Peter Fritz Walter, The Energy Nature of Human Emotions and Sexual Attraction (2015/2017).

Oedipal Reality means Cultural Slavery

Responsible parents raise their children in total opposition to Freud and the cultural slavery that his theories and the power structures of patriarchal society require, and give their children ample opportunity for peer-peer, and peer-adult, emotional and sexual relations, by interfering as little as possible in their children's love lives, which includes avoiding both emotional and sexual incest, while at the same time encouraging the child to project their libido upon figures outside of the family framework.

OEDIPAL CULTURE

CASTRATION OR PERMISSIVENESS?

My criticism of *Oedipal Culture* is inextricably woven with my critique of Sigmund Freud's 'cultural' concept of psychoanalysis, and here especially my revision of his theory of the *Oedipus Complex*.

Many young parents believe psychoanalysis had contributed to the liberation of the child; they tend to think it was a professional vintage of *permissiveness*, or a variant of *permissive education*. Nothing could be farther from the truth. Freudian psychoanalysis, applied to children is not permissive, it is normative; it is actually a tool for forging the ideal consumer child within a consumer culture based upon ordained consumption. As such, it is an ideological pillar for the functioning of a society that, as a matter of economic necessity, needs to repress natural pleasure because it replaces it by *consumer pleasure*.

Psychoanalysis is not permissive at all. It can be proven statistically that the word most used in psychoanalytic publications is the word *castration*.

Castration is a highly violent term that suggests the cutting off of the male sexual organ or the infibulation of the female sexual organ, the latter often also being called *clitoridectomy*. While psychoanalysis suggests to use a mythical or metaphorical vocabulary, this vocabulary becomes strangely real when it goes to take a measure that will affect the long-term destiny of a child or a family. In discarding out children who are judged as *sex offenders* or social delinquents, psychoanalysis exerts its full social power in that it can put people, not only adults, but also children, in jail. The children's jails are cutely called educational rehabilitation centers, but their regulating principles are the same as those of jails for adults, however with the difference that in child jails to this very day constitutional principles are not applied, while those principles are well in place for adult prisons.

This shows, more than anything else, the true attitude of *Oedipal Culture* toward children, as it shows the devil's face of this matter called *child protection*.

Are Masturbating Children Better Citizens?

Françoise Dolto, the late French child therapist and psychoanalyst was very outspoken about the benefits of masturbation but I interject that we are not set in the world to masturbate, but to *copulate* and lovingly embrace others.

We are not set in the world to engage in endless autoerotic self-satisfaction, but to use our natural erotic desire for building *relationships*. In this sense, sexuality is social, a social factor, and social behavior. Hence, people who are sexual are more social than those who repress their sexual wishes.

Child development, as a whole, today cunningly cheats about this fact and relegates the child to *eternal masturbation in the name of their own best.*

Children are encouraged to develop the habit of masturbation, instead of learning to make love with another human, which is the real, and natural, form of loving sexual embrace. What a split paradigm this is! The child is encouraged to be autoerotic, which means narcissistic, and to develop erotic fixations upon their parents, but violently, with all the police power of modern society, withheld from engaging in what is most natural: to embrace others lovingly, others who are not incestuous objects, and thus peer children and adults other than their parents.

Sorry, I believe that Western culture's child-rearing paradigm, whatever Dolto and others had and have to say about it, is perverse, as it really puts life upside down in the name of culture, morality or whatever other fake arguments. Dolto encourages professionals to take note of the child's sexuality to better serve the child, but what does this service look like down the road? To transform loving children into egoistic masturbators and incestuously fixated psychopaths?

The functional organic troubles of children she mentions in her books are often the result of *love prohibitions*, not prohibitions to masturbate, but prohibitions to have real love relations outside of the family, and to have the basic freedom to build such love relations in the first place. See the following quote from *Psychanalyse et Pédiatrie (1971)*:

> All those who study behavior problems, functional organic troubles, the educators, the doctors in the true sense of the term, must have notions about the role of libidinal life and know that sexual education is the grain for the social adaptation of the individual. (Id., 63, Translation mine)

It is of course true what Dolto says about the negative effects of *prohibiting* masturbation. But the trick is that the reverse argumentation is not per se correct. To allow masturbation does not mean to per se give the child *real freedom* for love. This is the logic error here, and here is where society cheats the child and argues from an irrational and mystical position that is not factually verifiable. The prototype example for this mysticism is where society or psychoanalysis—and here they lovingly coincide in their spanking the consumer child— speak about *pedophilia* when the question is not giving pedophiles their right, but giving children their right to love adults. These are two different matters, do what you will, but they are thrown in one pot and judged as one and the same thing. Here is exactly where the trail of lies begins. Dolto writes:

> To prohibit the child to masturbate and sexual curiosity means to force the child to pay unnecessary attention to activities and which normally, before puberty, are unconscious or preconscious. (…) Developing consciousness prematurely in an atmosphere of guilt does great harm to the development of the child because it deprives the child of ways to use their vital energies (libido) that is inherent in those spontaneous activities. Psychically healthy children who have mastered the genital stage are toilet-trained, graceful in their body and dexterous with their hands, they talk well, listen and observe a lot, like to imitate what they see others doing, ask questions and expect truthful answers, and when they don't receive them, begin to make up magical explanations. (Id., 66, Translation mine)

> The truth is that normal masturbation does not at all fatigue the child, but appeases the phallic vital tension of which give his erections ample evidence. Masturbation provides the child with physiological and affective relaxation which does not equal in intensity the orgasm of an adult as there is no ejaculation (…) (Id., 70, Translation mine)

The Dogma of the Autoerotic Consumer Child

It goes without saying that for those who are against all expressions of children's eroticism, Dolto's ideas about child masturbation must sound somewhat progressive or permissive. But from the background of the larger picture that I am trying to paint here, masturbation, while it's good of course and while many children need it just for getting rid of their surplus bioenergetic charge, is not the *real thing* what the child needs and asks for. To repeat it, we are born to learn copulating, not masturbating, and what children should learn instead of becoming proud masturbators is to become humble partners in a real sexual embrace where set and setting are correct, and where there is mutual respect, dignity, love and acceptance.

To say this, excuse me, is not an apology for *pedophilia*, as such a social policy, once enacted, would naturally lead, just as in most native cultures, to sexual relations among children.

If a random number of children choose adult mates, this then has to be respected, for there can only be *one* result when we give the child the right for free choice relations. If children are free to choose their mates, they must be allowed to have adult partners as well. To do so does not imply a legal implementation of pedophilia as a new social and legal paradigm, let me be explicit about this!

However, it well implies that there is no criminal punishment for adults who engage in sexual relations with consenting children. But as matters are in our culture, the basic resistance against children as erotic beings is not even child-adult sexual interaction, but even more so, child-child sexual interaction. According to Freud's cultural preservation theory, to admit and endorse child-child sexual relations is against the setup of our culture.

This dogmatic position of Freud is documented and led to a number of conflicts with his students. It was the main reason for Wilhelm Reich taking a distance to Freud, after the latter said regarding Reich's activism for the sexual liberation of children 'Culture must prevail!'

Françoise Dolto, when I interviewed her in 1986 in Paris, put it in the following terms:

> It is true that Freud was normative in this matter. But why not? The task of psychoanalysis is not to

> bring about a social revolution or changing the cultural paradigm. We are here as psychoanalysts to heal the neurosis, in the individual case, that comes from the cultural repression of the child's sexuality. This is our task, not more and not less. Freud has seen it in the same way. (Quoted from memory. Translation mine)

Hordes of slave-psychoanalysts follow their master in this greatest myth of all myths that Freud created with the whole of his doctrine of the *Oedipus Complex*. It may be against our tradition to eventually accept the child's full sexual freedom, but every culture can change, and only when it's in constant change, it's alive. *A culture that never changes is a dead culture, and a dead culture is a no-culture.*

In truth, what Freud ordained here as some kind of cultural imperative was a command to uphold patriarchy, so he was not that progressive child-loving psychoanalyst that history has made out of him, but a reactionary! And his doctrine, then, is a recipe for cultural neurosis and stagnation, not for cultural progress.

The advice Françoise Dolto gives to parents for the child who is found to masturbate often is equally ambiguous, and suspiciously on the line of Freud's cultural reasoning.

She argues such a child would have to be *initiated*. And until here I agree. But she continues that such a child has to be initiated into superior activities, which require a higher mental level than those usually reserved for children of that age.

> [W]hen you see a child masturbating often, a child who is normal, you can be certain it's a gifted child that should be initiated into superior activities, which require a higher mental level than those usually reserved for children of that age. But even more often, it's a neurotic child for whom masturbation has become an obsessional habit. Such a child must be given treatment, not punishment. To intimidate the child, or even prohibit masturbation will impair the development of the child; in case the child obeys the prohibition he will become dull and insensitive, and if he does not obey he will become unstable, angry, undisciplined and revolted. Neither of this is intended to be brought about by the adults who react in those ways; but this is what adults are doing to children, without knowing what they are doing. (Psychanalyse et Pédiatrie (1971), 74. Translation mine)

INTELLECT BOOSTING FOR SEXUALLY DEMANDING CHILDREN

That means a child who is longing for stronger sexual fulfillment than that of masturbation has to receive a *boost of their intellect*. That is really giving a child a pear who asks for an apple. What such a child naturally wants is to be initiated into loving copulation, because in masturbation, as my research on the human energy field clearly shows, the vital energy level is well brought to a new balance through orgasm, but that is not all there is in sexual love.

What is perhaps even more essential than the sexual abreaction is the *tactile experience* of two nude bodies being close in excitation for a while, which results in a high-level exchange of bioelectricity and emotional flow which is like feeding our internal batteries, strengthening our immune system and working counter to the aging process. From this larger picture that I tried to paint here, the pretended revolution of so-called infantile sexuality sounds like a bad joke, if it was not a bad trick, and actually a big lie and a real enslavement of the child in the name of a life-denying dead culture that knows only to consume and to possess, and as a result, to conquer and to rape, but not to live and to love and respectfully embrace.

Of course, what Dolto reasons here about the development of the rational mind is all true; it's genitality that brings about the objective mind. But our society is not a group of genitally developed individuals, which is why it is so deeply irrational and mystical, and so little responsible. Our society is one of anally fixated fabulators who are caught in the trap of mysticism that they call, in their madness, *psychoanalysis*.

To take an ideological crap science and culture-protection system such as psychoanalysis for the ultimate truth about life or childhood is about the greatest madness I have ever heard of in my life. What Dolto says in the following quotes is valid even more for *real genital cultures* such as the Trobriand islands where children learn to copulate from early age, and not, as in our culture, to become virtuous masturbators and pleasing night cushions for their emotionally frustrated parents. The difference is that they do not need the whole of the Oedipal construct, with its detour to arrive at genitality and heterosexuality *via homosexuality,* simply because they give real freedom to their children, and real sexuality, not a perverted form of it. And that is why the outcome is *real heterosexuality,* and not, as in our culture, fake heterosexuality.

> It is only *after the liquidation of the Oedipus* that thought can be put at the service of so-called altruistic sexuality, which means that seeking narcissistic satisfactions must have been overcome, without however invalidating those satisfactions. In the genital state, thought is characterized by common sense, prudence, and objective observation. It's what we call rational thought. (Id., 54, Translation mine)

QUALIFYING OEDIPAL CASTRATION AS CHILD ABUSE?

My criticism of Dolto, as I was on good terms with her and exchanged with her for a while, may sound strange and exaggerated, but it is not in any way directed against her personally. I am speaking here about the perversity of the whole of psychoanalysis, the whole theater and comedy it represents, the grotesque family scenarios it plans and puts on stage, and the whole abstruse worldview it embodies.

What Dolto explains in the following quotes is certainly true, sadly true, as it exactly shows the shadow side of the whole of the Oedipal construct, and what it results in when the boy does not make it to 'liquidate his Oedipus,' as psychoanalysts express it. And yes, the problem is more stringent with boys than with girls, for reasons we do not yet fully understand, but it has been argued by many psychologists that men generally are psychically more fragile than women.

> There are boys who stay lovingly fixated upon their mothers; their behavior is characterized by the fact that they do not attempt to 'seduce' any other woman. If the father is alive, the two men are constantly disputing, for the fact that the boy does not detach himself from his mother and searches out other love and sex objects proves that the boy has not liquidated—in a friendship of equality with his father—his pre-oedipal homosexuality. He will therefore prepare for getting 'in trouble' with his father through his difficult and provocative behavior. (Id., 88, Translation mine)

> When the father has left and the boy 'dedicates himself' to his mother, this behavior can be accompanied by real social sublimations, which are associated with the activities derived from the repression of genital and procreative sexuality, but this boy cannot behave sexually and affectively like an adult. He suffers from inferiority feelings toward men that he unconsciously identifies with his father; he can also be a hyper-genital who is always avid to get new sex partners toward whom he will never build real attachment, but he will show impotent in relations with any woman he really loves, because this is associated in his unconscious with the tabooed incestuous object. (Id., 88-89, Translation mine)

> This is how the superego of the boy becomes very early rigid (…); the reason for this is the necessity to repress the heterosexual desire in the 'maternal sphere' (Id., 89, Translation mine)

The *symbiotic fixation* upon a parent, especially the mother, beyond the natural mother-infant symbiosis, and thus after the age of 18 months of the infant, is *pathological* and it brings about a clear reduction of intelligence because of the entanglement of the vital energies of parent and child. This is particularly true, as Dolto, points it out, in the mother-son relation, and much less in the father-daughter relation because the mother-matrix has naturally a greater attraction power for the child than the father-spermgiver.

When mothers do not encourage their children to develop autonomy, they are on the best way to entangle their children in a codependence where the parent is the winner and the child the loser, and where the child, in most cases without parent and child being really conscious about that, becomes the *ersatz-mate* for the parent. While this mating is in most cases not sexual, the consequences of mother-son codependence are devastating.

I talk about *emotional abuse* in cases where the parent has received clear signals from the child for being granted more freedom and autonomy, but does repeatedly not comply with this request, or even actively cuts down or prohibits love and erotic relations of the child with persons outside of the family, whatever their age.

Last not least, it doesn't come as a surprise when Dolto categorically judges perverse behavior and social delinquency as the result of a non-liquidated Oedipus, or one that is not yet liquidated.

> [P]erverse behavior or social delinquents, both are the result of a non-liquidated Oedipus, or a not yet liquidated one. (Id., 130, Translation mine)

RATIONALITY VS. OEDIPAL MYSTICISM

The judgmental attitude of psychoanalysis is not surprising; it shows how devastating the Oedipal construct is at the end of the day, together with all the cultural weed that has grown around it. This insight, that is shared by most psychoanalysts and psychiatrists is not the real bomb; the real bomb is the fact that our society tolerates psychiatric nonsense that perverts our children into potential violent perpetrators, using a construct for the psychosexual growth of our children that is anti-life, dysfunctional, dangerous and unnatural.

There must be an awakening one day; perhaps a movement is to be created that is similar to *Antipsychiatry* in that it clearly unveils the social utilitarianism of Oedipal Culture's child development paradigm because what it creates is not psychic health and responsible citizens but *emotional and sexual cripples* and a horde of silent anarchists who, while paying lip service to order and morality, are in fact barbarous uncivilized rapists because they have never ever learnt to copulate and embrace another in love when they were young and still open for sexual learning.

Modern rape research has shown that rapists are highly sexually inexperienced individuals who foster in most cases a highly repressive and moralistic worldview. These people suffer not from too much but from too little permissiveness and a blown-up super ego, and they are usually endorsing educational violence. In addition it has been shown that they are hostile toward healthy and caring touch, and suffer from actual tactile deprivation. It is for this reason correct when researchers on the roots of violence, such as Dr. James W. Prescott, suggest to treat sex offenders with sexual permissiveness, granting them relaxation, massage, psychotherapy and frequent loving sexual embrace.

> —See, for example, James W. Prescott, Body Pleasure and the Origins of Violence (1975) and Deprivation of Physical Affection as a Primary Process in the Development of Physical Violence, A Comparative and Cross-Cultural Perspective, in: David G. Gil, ed., Child Abuse and Violence (1979), pp. 77, 78.

Seen from a social policy point of view, we must conclude that it's exactly this denial of *real child sexuality* in the form of an active involvement of children in love relations outside of the family that renders our culture so outright false, morally corrupt, violent and destructive. And what we get from the pulpit of psychoanalysis here is but reject and denial, a false, jovial and grinning pseudo permissiveness which is an outright betrayal of the child, together with cathedral lectures from a blown-up patriarchal superego incarnated in women like Dolto, who 'speak the rude truth in all ways,' to paraphrase Emerson. Only that contrary to Emerson's, this truth does not liberate, but enchains our children in more codependence, more emotional entanglement and abuse and more murderous fascist ideologies to come from this soil of a deeply perverted psychosexual base structure, which is the rotten foundation of our culture.

OEDIPAL HERO

Oedipal Hero is a term I forged for an individual, usually of male sex, who suffers from a specific pathology that comes from a combination of unresolved *Oedipus Complex* and a narcissistic fixation. In my view, modern psychiatry has just begun to identify this problem, and my approach to scientifically and psychologically outline this pathology is therefore to be seen as a pioneering work.

> —See Peter Fritz Walter, Oedipal Hero: The Hidden Side of Glory (Scholarly Articles, Vol. 20), 2017.

I use the term *Oedipal Culture* or *Oedipal Consciousness* synonymously with a range of similar expressions so as to denote the complex process of denial of truth about the cyclic and pleasure-bound nature of life through the repression of the child's emonic vitality. Wilhelm Reich wrote in *Ether, God and Devil (1949/1972)*:

> The unarmored organism does not know an impulse to rape and murder little girls, or to get plea-

> sure through violence. It is therefore indifferent to-
> ward all moral rules that try to repress such impuls-
> es. It cannot comprehend that one has intercourse
> with another only because there is an opportunity
> for it, for example being in one and the same room
> with a person of the other sex. The armored charac-
> ter, by contrast, cannot envision an orderly life
> without coercive laws against rape and lust murder.

While the true reason for repressing the child's emotional vitality is hardly ever discussed in international consumer culture, the lifting of the veil behind so-called morality used to be a strong domain of post-revolution French philosophy.

Most people in modern consumer culture really believe the main reason for inhibiting the child's free sexuality had to do with morality or with a concern for protecting the child's natural vulnerability. This cultural and social naiveté strongly contrasts with other cultures' perspective, such as the French or Hispanic cultures, and it stringently contradicts the life and love philosophy of most tribal cultures.

French social historians such as Michel Foucault and social philosophers such as Gilles Deleuze have clearly demonstrated that the reasons for the child's emotional castration are to be found in the setup of Western consumer economy.

> —See Michel Foucault, The History of Sexuality, Vol. I : The Will to Knowledge (1976/1998), The History of Sexuality, Vol. II : The Use of Pleasure (1984/1998), The History of Sexuality, Vol. III : The Care of Self (1984/1998) and Gilles Deleuze, Gilles & Felix Guattari, L'Anti-Oedipe: Capitalisme et Schizophrénie (1973).

It has economic, and not moral reasons why the Western consumer child is relegated to forced orality and deprived of tactile stimulation.

Gilles Deleuze and Felix Guattari, in their philosophical exposé *Anti-Oedipus, Capitalism & Schizophrenia*, set out to formulate a detailed philosophical, logical and ethical critique of Freud's theory of the Oedipus Complex.

To illustrate my own point of view, subject to several of my books, I will provide here some quotes of this major philosophical and psychoanalytic treatise. All the quotes are my own translation from the French original.

> People often believe that with Oedipus, it's easy, and you can take that for granted. But it is not so: Oedipus presupposes an extraordinary repression of de-

siring machines. And why, and for what reason? (Id., 8)

Does Oedipal imperialism only require to abandon biological realism? Or has something else, infinitely more powerful, been sacrificed to Oedipus? (Id., 63)

The un-Oedipal nature of desire production contin-ues to exist, but is aligned with Oedipal coordinates that translate it in 'pre-Oedipal', 'para-Oedipal' or 'quasi-Oedipal,' etc. (Id., 65)

BIBLIOGRAPHY

Contextual Bibliography

ARIÈS, PHILIPPE

Centuries of Childhood
NEW YORK: VINTAGE BOOKS, 1962

ARNTZ, WILLIAM & CHASSE, BETSY

What the Bleep Do We Know
20TH CENTURY FOX, 2005 (DVD)

Down The Rabbit Hole Quantum Edition
20TH CENTURY FOX, 2006 (3 DVD SET)

COVITZ, JOEL

Emotional Child Abuse
THE FAMILY CURSE
BOSTON: SIGO PRESS, 1986

DeMause, Lloyd

The History of Childhood
NEW YORK, 1974

Foundations of Psychohistory
NEW YORK: CREATIVE ROOTS, 1982

Diamond, Stephen A., May, Rollo

Anger, Madness, and the Daimonic
THE PSYCHOLOGICAL GENESIS OF VIOLENCE, EVIL AND CREATIVITY
NEW YORK: STATE UNIVERSITY OF NEW YORK PRESS, 1999

DiCarlo, Russell E. (Ed.)

Towards A New World View
CONVERSATIONS AT THE LEADING EDGE
ERIE, PA: EPIC PUBLISHING, 1996

Dolto, Françoise

La Cause des Enfants
PARIS: LAFFONT, 1985

Psychanalyse et Pédiatrie
PARIS: SEUIL, 1971

Séminaire de Psychanalyse d'Enfants, 1
PARIS: SEUIL, 1982

Séminaire de Psychanalyse d'Enfants, 2
PARIS: SEUIL, 1985

Séminaire de Psychanalyse d'Enfants, 3
PARIS: SEUIL, 1988

L'évangile au risque de la psychanalyse
PARIS: SEUIL, 1980

EISLER, RIANE

The Chalice and the Blade
OUR HISTORY, OUR FUTURE
SAN FRANCISCO: HARPER & ROW, 1995

Sacred Pleasure: Sex, Myth and the Politics of the Body
NEW PATHS TO POWER AND LOVE
SAN FRANCISCO: HARPER & ROW, 1996

The Partnership Way
NEW TOOLS FOR LIVING AND LEARNING
WITH DAVID LOYE
BRANDON, VT: HOLISTIC EDUCATION PRESS, 1998

The Real Wealth of Nations
CREATING A CARING ECONOMICS
SAN FRANCISCO: BERRETT-KOEHLER PUBLISHERS, 2008

ELLIS, HAVELOCK

Sexual Inversion
REPUBLISHED
NEW YORK: UNIVERSITY PRESS OF THE PACIFIC, 2001
ORIGINALLY PUBLISHED IN 1897

The Sexual Impulse in Women
REPUBLISHED
NEW YORK: UNIVERSITY PRESS OF THE PACIFIC, 2001
ORIGINALLY PUBLISHED IN 1903

The Dance of Life
NEW YORK: GREENWOOD PRESS REPRINT EDITION, 1973
ORIGINALLY PUBLISHED IN 1923

ELWIN, V.

The Muria and their Ghotul
BOMBAY: OXFORD UNIVERSITY PRESS, 1947

ERICKSON, MILTON H.

My Voice Will Go With You
THE TEACHING TALES OF MILTON H. ERICKSON
BY SIDNEY ROSEN (ED.)
NEW YORK: NORTON & CO., 1991

Complete Works 1.0, CD-ROM
NEW YORK: MILTON H. ERICKSON FOUNDATION, 2001

FREUD, SIGMUND

The Interpretation of Dreams
NEW YORK: AVON, REISSUE EDITION, 1980
AND IN: THE STANDARD EDITION OF THE COMPLETE PSYCHOLOGICAL
WORKS OF SIGMUND FREUD , (24 VOLUMES) ED. BY JAMES STRACHEY
NEW YORK: W. W. NORTON & COMPANY, 1976

Totem and Taboo
NEW YORK: ROUTLEDGE, 1999
ORIGINALLY PUBLISHED IN 1913

FROMM, ERICH

The Anatomy of Human Destructiveness
NEW YORK: OWL BOOK, 1992
ORIGINALLY PUBLISHED IN 1973

Escape from Freedom
NEW YORK: OWL BOOKS, 1994
ORIGINALLY PUBLISHED IN 1941
TO HAVE OR TO BE
NEW YORK: CONTINUUM INTERNATIONAL PUBLISHING, 1996
ORIGINALLY PUBLISHED IN 1976

The Art of Loving
NEW YORK: HARPERPERENNIAL, 2000
ORIGINALLY PUBLISHED IN 1956

GOLEMAN, DANIEL

Emotional Intelligence
NEW YORK, BANTAM BOOKS, 1995

GORDON, ROSEMARY

Pedophilia: Normal and Abnormal
IN: KRAEMER, THE FORBIDDEN LOVE
LONDON, 1976

GOSWAMI, AMIT

The Self-Aware Universe
HOW CONSCIOUSNESS CREATES THE MATERIAL WORLD
NEW YORK: TARCHER/PUTNAM, 1995

GROTH, A. NICHOLAS

Men Who Rape
THE PSYCHOLOGY OF THE OFFENDER
NEW YORK: PERSEUS PUBLISHING, 1980

HAMEROFF, NEWBERG, WOOLF, BIERMAN

Consciousness
20 SCIENTISTS INTERVIEWED
DIRECTOR: GREGORY ALSBURY
5 DVD BOX SET, 540 MIN.
NEW YORK: ALSBURY FILMS, 2003

JAMES, WILLIAM

Writings 1902-1910
THE VARIETIES OF RELIGIOUS EXPERIENCE / PRAGMATISM / A PLURALISTIC UNI-
VERSE / THE MEANING OF TRUTH / SOME PROBLEMS OF PHILOSOPHY / ESSAYS
NEW YORK: LIBRARY OF AMERICA, 1988

Jung, Carl Gustav

Archetypes of the Collective Unconscious
IN: THE BASIC WRITINGS OF C.G. JUNG
NEW YORK: THE MODERN LIBRARY, 1959, 358-407

Collected Works
NEW YORK, 1959

On the Nature of the Psyche
IN: THE BASIC WRITINGS OF C.G. JUNG
NEW YORK: THE MODERN LIBRARY, 1959, 47-133

Psychological Types
COLLECTED WRITINGS, VOL. 6
PRINCETON: PRINCETON UNIVERSITY PRESS, 1971

Psychology and Religion
IN: THE BASIC WRITINGS OF C.G. JUNG
NEW YORK: THE MODERN LIBRARY, 1959, 582-655

Religious and Psychological Problems of Alchemy
IN: THE BASIC WRITINGS OF C.G. JUNG
NEW YORK: THE MODERN LIBRARY, 1959, 537-581

The Basic Writings of C.G. Jung
NEW YORK: THE MODERN LIBRARY, 1959

The Development of Personality
COLLECTED WRITINGS, VOL. 17
PRINCETON: PRINCETON UNIVERSITY PRESS, 1954

The Meaning and Significance of Dreams
BOSTON: SIGO PRESS, 1991

The Myth of the Divine Child
IN: ESSAYS ON A SCIENCE OF MYTHOLOGY
PRINCETON, N.J.: PRINCETON UNIVERSITY PRESS BOLLINGEN
SERIES XXII, 1969. (WITH KARL KERENYI)

Two Essays on Analytical Psychology
COLLECTED WRITINGS, VOL. 7
PRINCETON: PRINCETON UNIVERSITY PRESS, 1972
FIRST PUBLISHED BY ROUTLEDGE & KEGAN PAUL, LTD., 1953

KLEIN, MELANIE

Love, Guilt and Reparation, and Other Works 1921-1945
NEW YORK: FREE PRESS, 1984
(REISSUE EDITION)

Envy and Gratitude and Other Works 1946-1963
NEW YORK: FREE PRESS, 2002
(REISSUE EDITION)

KOESTLER, ARTHUR

The Act of Creation
NEW YORK: PENGUIN ARKANA, 1989.
ORIGINALLY PUBLISHED IN 1964

KRISHNAMURTI, J.

Freedom From The Known
SAN FRANCISCO: HARPER & ROW, 1969

The First and Last Freedom
SAN FRANCISCO: HARPER & ROW, 1975

Education and the Significance of Life
LONDON: VICTOR GOLLANCZ, 1978

CONTEXTUAL BIBLIOGRAPHY

Commentaries on Living
FIRST SERIES
LONDON: VICTOR GOLLANCZ, 1985

Commentaries on Living
SECOND SERIES
LONDON: VICTOR GOLLANCZ, 1986

Krishnamurti's Journal
LONDON: VICTOR GOLLANCZ, 1987

Krishnamurti's Notebook
LONDON: VICTOR GOLLANCZ, 1986

Beyond Violence
LONDON: VICTOR GOLLANCZ, 1985

Beginnings of Learning
NEW YORK: PENGUIN, 1986

The Penguin Krishnamurti Reader
NEW YORK: PENGUIN, 1987

On God
SAN FRANCISCO: HARPER & ROW, 1992

On Fear
SAN FRANCISCO: HARPER & ROW, 1995

The Essential Krishnamurti
SAN FRANCISCO: HARPER & ROW, 1996

The Ending of Time
WITH DR. DAVID BOHM
SAN FRANCISCO: HARPER & ROW, 1985

LAING, RONALD DAVID

Divided Self
NEW YORK: VIKING PRESS, 1991

R.D. Laing and the Paths of Anti-Psychiatry
ED., BY Z. KOTOWICZ
LONDON: ROUTLEDGE, 1997

The Politics of Experience
NEW YORK: PANTHEON, 1983

LIEDLOFF, JEAN

Continuum Concept
IN SEARCH OF HAPPINESS LOST
NEW YORK: PERSEUS BOOKS, 1986
FIRST PUBLISHED IN 1977

LOWEN, ALEXANDER

Bioenergetics
NEW YORK: COWARD, MCGOEGHAM 1975

Depression and the Body
THE BIOLOGICAL BASIS OF FAITH AND REALITY
NEW YORK: PENGUIN, 1992

Fear of Life
NEW YORK: BIOENERGETIC PRESS, 2003

Honoring the Body
THE AUTOBIOGRAPHY OF ALEXANDER LOWEN
NEW YORK: BIOENERGETIC PRESS, 2004

Joy
THE SURRENDER TO THE BODY AND TO LIFE

NEW YORK: PENGUIN, 1995

Love and Orgasm
NEW YORK: MACMILLAN, 1965

Love, Sex and Your Heart
NEW YORK: BIOENERGETICS PRESS, 2004

Narcissism: Denial of the True Self
NEW YORK: MACMILLAN, COLLIER BOOKS, 1983

Pleasure: A Creative Approach to Life
NEW YORK: BIOENERGETICS PRESS, 2004
FIRST PUBLISHED IN 1970

The Language of the Body
PHYSICAL DYNAMICS OF CHARACTER STRUCTURE
NEW YORK: BIOENERGETICS PRESS, 2006

MILLER, ALICE

Four Your Own Good
HIDDEN CRUELTY IN CHILD-REARING AND THE ROOTS OF VIOLENCE
NEW YORK: FARRAR, STRAUS & GIROUX, 1983

Pictures of a Childhood
NEW YORK: FARRAR, STRAUS & GIROUX, 1986

The Drama of the Gifted Child
IN SEARCH FOR THE TRUE SELF
TRANSLATED BY RUTH WARD
NEW YORK: BASIC BOOKS, 1996

Thou Shalt Not Be Aware
SOCIETY'S BETRAYAL OF THE CHILD
NEW YORK: NOONDAY, 1998

The Political Consequences of Child Abuse
IN: THE JOURNAL OF PSYCHOHISTORY 26, 2 (FALL 1998)

MOORE, THOMAS

Care of the Soul
A GUIDE FOR CULTIVATING DEPTH AND SACREDNESS IN EVERYDAY LIFE
NEW YORK: HARPER & COLLINS, 1994

REICH, WILHELM

Children of the Future
ON THE PREVENTION OF SEXUAL PATHOLOGY
NEW YORK: FARRAR, STRAUS & GIROUX, 1983
FIRST PUBLISHED IN 1950

CORE (Cosmic Orgone Engineering)
PART I, SPACE SHIPS, DOR AND DROUGHT
©1984, ORGONE INSTITUTE PRESS
XEROX COPY FROM THE WILHELM REICH MUSEUM

Early Writings 1
NEW YORK: FARRAR, STRAUS & GIROUX, 1975

Ether, God & Devil & Cosmic Superimposition
NEW YORK: FARRAR, STRAUS & GIROUX, 1972
ORIGINALLY PUBLISHED IN 1949

Genitality in the Theory and Therapy of Neurosis
©1980 BY MARY BOYD HIGGINS AS DIRECTOR OF THE WILHELM REICH INFANT
TRUST

People in Trouble

CONTEXTUAL BIBLIOGRAPHY

©1974 BY MARY BOYD HIGGINS AS DIRECTOR OF THE WILHELM REICH INFANT TRUST

Record of a Friendship
THE CORRESPONDENCE OF WILHELM REICH AND A. S. NEILL
NEW YORK, FARRAR, STRAUS & GIROUX, 1981

Selected Writings
AN INTRODUCTION TO ORGONOMY
NEW YORK: FARRAR, STRAUS & GIROUX, 1973

The Bioelectrical Investigation of Sexuality and Anxiety
NEW YORK: FARRAR, STRAUS & GIROUX, 1983
ORIGINALLY PUBLISHED IN 1935

The Bion Experiments
REPRINTED IN *SELECTED WRITINGS*
NEW YORK: FARRAR, STRAUS & GIROUX, 1973

The Function of the Orgasm (The Orgone, Vol. 1)
ORGONE INSTITUTE PRESS, NEW YORK, 1942

The Cancer Biopathy (The Orgone, Vol. 2)
NEW YORK: FARRAR, STRAUS & GIROUX, 1973

The Invasion of Compulsory Sex Morality
NEW YORK: FARRAR, STRAUS & GIROUX, 1971
ORIGINALLY PUBLISHED IN 1932

The Leukemia Problem: Approach
©1951, ORGONE INSTITUTE PRESS
COPYRIGHT RENEWED 1979
XEROX COPY FROM THE WILHELM REICH MUSEUM

The Mass Psychology of Fascism
NEW YORK: FARRAR, STRAUS & GIROUX, 1970
ORIGINALLY PUBLISHED IN 1933

The Orgone Energy Accumulator
ITS SCIENTIFIC AND MEDICAL USE
©1951, 1979, ORGONE INSTITUTE PRESS

XEROX COPY FROM THE WILHELM REICH MUSEUM

The Schizophrenic Split
©1945, 1949, 1972 BY MARY BOYD HIGGINS AS DIRECTOR OF THE
WILHELM REICH INFANT TRUST
XEROX COPY FROM THE WILHELM REICH MUSEUM

The Sexual Revolution
©1945, 1962 BY MARY BOYD HIGGINS AS DIRECTOR OF THE WILHELM REICH
INFANT TRUST

REID, DANIEL P.

The Tao of Health, Sex & Longevity
A MODERN PRACTICAL GUIDE TO THE ANCIENT WAY
NEW YORK: SIMON & SCHUSTER, 1989

Guarding the Three Treasures
THE CHINESE WAY OF HEALTH
NEW YORK: SIMON & SCHUSTER, 1993

ROSEN, SYDNEY (ED.)

My Voice Will Go With You
THE TEACHING TALES OF MILTON H. ERICKSON
NEW YORK: NORTON & CO., 1991

STEIN, ROBERT M.

Redeeming the Inner Child in Marriage and Therapy
IN: RECLAIMING THE INNER CHILD
ED. BY JEREMIAH ABRAMS
NEW YORK: TARCHER/PUTNAM, 1990, 261 FF.

STEINER, RUDOLF

Theosophy
AN INTRODUCTION TO THE SPIRITUAL PROCESSES IN HUMAN LIFE
AND IN THE COSMOS
NEW YORK: ANTHROPOSOPHIC PRESS, 1994

STONE, HAL & STONE, SIDRA

Embracing Our Selves
THE VOICE DIALOGUE MANUAL
SAN RAFAEL, CA: NEW WORLD LIBRARY, 1989

SZASZ, THOMAS

The Myth of Mental Illness
NEW YORK: HARPER & ROW, 1984

TART, CHARLES T.

Altered States of Consciousness
A BOOK OF READINGS
HOBOKEN, N.J.: WILEY & SONS, 1969

WHAT THE BLEEP DO WE KNOW!?

See Arntz, William

WHITFIELD, CHARLES L.

Healing the Child Within
DEERFIELD BEACH, FL: HEALTH COMMUNICATIONS, 1987

PERSONAL NOTES